Winter in a River Beach Town

poems by

Ruth Ann Allaire

Finishing Line Press
Georgetown, Kentucky

Winter in a River Beach Town

Copyright © 2016 by Ruth Ann Allaire
ISBN 978-1-944899-34-9 First Edition
All rights reserved under International and Pan-American Copyright Conventions.
No part of this book may be reproduced in any manner whatsoever without written permission from the publisher, except in the case of brief quotations embodied in critical articles and reviews.

ACKNOWLEDGMENTS

"Distinctions" and "Testament" *Northern Virginia Review*

Editor: Christen Kincaid

Cover Art: George Hickle Garland

Author Photo: Teresa Mohme

Cover Design: Elizabeth Maines

Printed in the USA on acid-free paper.
Order online: www.finishinglinepress.com
also available on amazon.com

Author inquiries and mail orders:
Finishing Line Press
P. O. Box 1626
Georgetown, Kentucky 40324
U. S. A.

Table of Contents

Too Soon 1

Perspective 2

Circling 3

November 4

Testament 5

Time 6

Reality 7

Rain trickles tonight 8

Sufficiency? 9

Vigil for the night 10

Observation # 3 11

Winter Warriors 12

Visions of the Paleocene 13

Snow Lies on My Heart 14

Depression 15

Clarity 16

Day and Night 17

Good Oak Wood 18

Diatribe 19

Distinctions 20

Winter Solstice 21

Differences 22

Hyacinths 24

Spice bush 25

*This book is dedicated to those
who walk the beach in winter,
alone,
with their thoughts, musings and ideas,
to say nothing,
of their memories.*

Too Soon

It came early this year,
the snow, I mean.
I heard it in your voice.

The leaves are not off the trees
and you are talking about next year.
We will go to Nantucket in August, you said.

The fall semesters are difficult,
Something about being overextended,
the pressures of work and commitment, you said.

Perhaps, sometime at Christmas,
spring break might be nice,
but when is that darn convention, you said.

These summers mean so much,
a chance to regroup and relax,
recharge the old batteries, you said.

But I had stopped listening;
I only heard the geese,
felt the snow on the green peach leaf.

The geese were headed
in other directions
and so were you.

Perspective

Autumn, again,
you have splashed color in my eyes
and left an iridescent film
of beauty hanging there.

I am not so easily beguiled;
for I have danced, autumn,
with your opalescent leaves before.

I have floated through the sky
on amber sails of poplar trees
and warmed my soul
at the holy incandescence
of black gum in the fall.

I have stood straight and proud
with the beaten bronze soldiers
of oaks on the mountainside
and clung with the last emerald leaf
until the willow struck her flags.

I have fallen to my knees
in the wind whipped pot
of maple gold and spent the winter
nestled on the ground
mid the twisted ecru tatter of the beech.

So, you cannot deceive me, autumn.
I may note the beauty
of your quilting and your gauze
but I have seen the shades
that wait within.

Circling

Catching all updrafts
falcons drift south, ignoring
leaves spiraling down.

November

The view is clearer now.
The gauzy leaves have dropped
like garments to the ground.
Black boles of trees stand out,
bleak and true,
against the opening
of a wider sky.

Testament

Brown and dry,
the reeds reply
to the winter's cold.

A testament
to the summer spent
and the right
to stand inviolate
and let
the winter wind of hate
surmount
but not destroy.

What roots
to hold the withered reed,
the withered reed,
so fast.

Time

and what of the wind that topples us all,
that topples the reeds in the marsh,
that flails at the frailest of stems?

and what of the water that seeps on us all,
that seeps from the quietest spring,
that erodes away every side?

and what of the wind, the water and time,
the time that creeps on us all
that topples us each, everyone?

Reality

A whisper rustled
outside the kitchen window.
My neighbor, I thought,
but the hour was late?
I opened the door.

There in the quiet road
in the soft, silver light
last year's bronze oak leaves
were dancing around.

The wind, you will say.

But I recognize
whirling dervishes in trance
when I see them.

Rain trickles tonight

over old eaves and fresh cracks
seeking new descents.

Sufficiency?

Can I stack enough oak
to keep the chill of winter
outside the door at night?

So many chunks of wood
and even more of memories
are vested in each tree.

The strength to split each log
is resting in my arms
and my arms are fragile now.

This pile of wood seems small.

Vigil for the night

Stoic
seagull
solitary
sentinel
standing
still on
sepia sand.

Withdrawn
within
whitewashed
wings
watching
with the
 wind-whipped waves.

Observation # 3

The owl flew in last night
and hung his silhouette
in the lightning struck old tree.

The mouse crept outward in the cold.
Since he was so anxious
no shadows did he see.

I watched both seekers in the dark,
innocent as I could be
but felt what the hungry see.

Winter Warriors

Naked branches
shriven
of extraneous foliage,
exposed
to the wind,
bending
to forces
not of their making.

Naked branches,
resilient spears,
withstanding,
resisting,
piercing the sky
in return.

Visions of the Paleocene

Walking on the beach,
you and I,
looking for fossils,
exposed by a river
cutting down
to an ancient sea,

You showed to me
a choice specimen
of alligator vertebrae.

Sixty five million
years erupted
before my eyes.

My insignificance
ascended in my mind,
until I,
like any dying thing,
grappled for your hand.

Snow Lies on My Heart

Snow lies on my heart tonight,
chills my blood like river ice,
distorts my life with silver white,
hides my dreams but not their price.

Depression

A new time for glaciers,
for ice encompassing the mind,
for eskers and arêtes,
for moraines in which to sink
even more ancient boulders of despair
deep within the sediments,
a new age for withdrawal
from hearth and friend;
a time for snow and silence.

Clarity

A lone bird's nest in a winter tree
sits starkly clear for the world to see,
a holding cup for the summer past
simply stating that some things last.

Day and Night

To grasp the dawn,
one needs more than icicles,
those crystal fingers of stiffening light
which soften and shrink with the warming day.

But night, ah, night,
helps each finger to extend its lucid tip
to spear and to stab
the encompassing chill.

Good Oak Wood

The night is streaking toward the dawn;
the owl is sliding through the trees.
With good oak wood
I have banked the morning's fire
down upon my knees.

Diatribe

Walking in the snow
we stopped to listen
to a tail dancing a jig squirrel,
sitting on a branch
and scolding a marauding jay,
who, by squawking back,
kept the argument going,
just like us.

Distinctions

For an ephemeral time
our four footprints scarred
the new fallen snow
until subsequent storms
filled in and sculpted
on the old impressions
our separate steps into
disproportionately
large and grotesque
markers of ourselves.

Our separateness was
blurred at last and lost
as the eventual blizzard
covered up our individual mounds.

Winter Solstice

Snow scattering
the tatterings of dried leaves
clinging to young beeches,
shattering these drenched druids'
garments before the spring.

Sleet splattering
among gnattering sparrow birds,
winging through sycamores,
battering these aged sorcerers
to break before the spring

Differences

You came by today,
not out of your way
and offered a ride
in your car.
I knew when
you glanced at your watch
that we would not
go very far,
so I said—
Let's go to the beach,
it's been out of reach
for so long while the river
kept the sand locked under ice
it usually wasn't nice
enough. It's such a relief
to be out in the sun.
And the first shell
I saw was the one that
really mattered
among those scattered
on that little section of reef.
and then a fine shark's tooth
though shattered
on one edge was still
incredibly good and will
go home to my collection
of teeth and bones
and other debris
and be kept out of reach
of curious hands.

I dug up some shoots
of lilies that were held
by the roots
of the indigo shrub felled
as it was by old vines
and twisted and tipped
by the wind and the lines
of tumbling sands.
And then a glorious chunk of wood
with knots like the eyes
of some sleepy, bound
owl which had been trapped
and then drowned
on the beach by the tide.

I sighed,
but way up ahead
I saw a thorn
with tips turning red,
a branch of which would be so
good for the stem of the boy's
much wanted candy tree
which I make each year
with chocolate eggs
and I saw by the way
that your legs
were heading that just
as I feared
it is time to go
so I scrambled together

two more shells
and a strip of bark
pushed above the drift
line by the melting new snow.
On the way home
blue birds high on the wire
irridescent feathers set afire
by the rays of the sun
and a golden patch
of poverty grass
showing some green at the base
of each stalk locked in place
by the seed bearing shaft
of the old.
When we got to my house
I unloaded your car
of all that I
had found on that bar,
the trivial treasures
gleaned from the sands
but I noticed that you
had nothing
to fill up your hands
although I know
you had walked by my side.
but anyway,
thanks for the ride.

Hyacinths

The ground is cold this morning,
damp and sour, not like yesterday,
when the sun coaxed forsythia
into dancing in the chilly air
and hyacinths into throwing away
their winter wraps.

I might as well go outside,
lie down with the hyacinths
and smell the odor of spring
for my bed is cold this morning,
empty and still, not like yesterday.

Spice bush

A slim wand of sweetened buds
holding tightly furled wings
against the tenacity of winter
and the awesome ease of spring.

Ruth Ann Allaire, Ph.D., is a retired college biology professor, who lives in Fredericksburg, VA. She is active in writing, genealogy research and studying various healing modalities. Married to an Egyptian she is interested in studying cultural differences. She volunteers for Virginia Master Naturalists.

George Hickle Garland (1944-1983) was an artist, having studied at Maryland Institute of Art before his illness. He employed pen and ink drawings to portray life around him. Sometimes stylistic, his simple lines brought the viewer into his world.

www.ingramcontent.com/pod-product-compliance
Lightning Source LLC
Chambersburg PA
CBHW060226050426
42446CB00013B/3194